A 30-DAY DEVOTIONAL

CONTRARY WINDS

Overcoming Fear to Experience the Abundant Life

Dr. LeSette M. Wright

All scriptures quoted in this book are from the New American Standard Bible (NASB) version unless otherwise indicated.
NKJV – New King James Version
NIV – New International Version
KJV –King James Version

All poetry written by LeSette M. Wright.

All acronyms used in this book were created by the author unless otherwise noted.

First printing edition 2018.

ISBN: 978-0-692-10216-9

Printed in the United States of America.

Dedication

I have come that they may have life, and that they may have it
more abundantly.
JOHN 10:10b (NKJV)

This book is dedicated to the Glory of God and to you.
Jesus came that you might have life and have it more
abundantly. God longs for you to live an exceedingly
great life, now and for all eternity. As the winds of life
rage against you, know that God "has not given you a
spirit of fear; but of power, and of love, and of a sound
mind."[1] As a child of God, contrary winds come not to
defeat you but to propel you into your abundant life!

With special thanks to the matriarchs for giving me the courage and inspiration to write.

In Loving Memory
of
Rosetta Royster Wright

A woman who fears (honors, reverences, worships) the Lord,
she shall be praised!
PROVERBS 31:30b KJV

Contents

Introduction

Over the years, I have spent time reflecting on the power and significance of fear. I have seen fear enslave people until their marriages are crippled, businesses are destroyed, hopes are dashed, and dreams are shattered. In the wake of the September 11 tragedies in the U.S., we witnessed fear's crippling impact on the world. We wondered if we would ever feel safe in airplanes again, or in our offices, on subways, at public gatherings. And to this day, some have not returned to that feeling of safety and some never will. Why?

Fear's grasp is relentless. It will not let go willingly. It must be ordered to vacate the premises. Too many of us have allowed fear to set up residence in our hearts and lives. Well, get ready to be set free. This book is a love letter to every child of God; a letter beseeching His beloved to no longer be enslaved by fear.

In the book of Exodus, chapters 14–15, we find Israel's deliverance at the Red Sea. Contained therein is a beautiful framework and exciting strategy for the deliverance of God's people from fear. This strategy is threefold:

1. When Fear Speaks, Cry Out to God!
    (Exodus 14:10–12)
2. As God Answers, Learn His Ways!
    (Exodus 14:13–31)
3. As you Learn His Ways, Sing Your Song!
    (Exodus 15:1–21).

Part I
When Fear Speaks, Cry Out To God!

And when Pharaoh drew near, the children of Israel lifted their eyes, and behold, the Egyptians marched after them. So they were very afraid, and the children of Israel cried out to the LORD. Then they said to Moses, "Because there were no graves in Egypt, have you taken us away to die in the wilderness? Why have you so dealt with us, to bring us up out of Egypt? Is this not the word that we told you in Egypt, saying, 'Let us alone that we may serve the Egyptians?' For it would have been better for us to serve the Egyptians than that we should die in the wilderness."
EXODUS 14:10–12 NKJV

As you can see from this passage, the children of Israel were overcome with fear. They turned on their leader and were so panic stricken that they felt it would have been better if they had stayed in slavery in Egypt. Perhaps you can relate to the Israelites' state of panic. Have you ever been overcome by fear and driven to delirium? In your journey through this book, Days 1–3 will challenge you to reflect on the role fear has played in your life.

Part II
As God Answers, Learn His Ways!

And Moses said to the people, "Do not be afraid. Stand still, and
see the salvation of the LORD, which He will accomplish for you
today. For the Egyptians whom you see today, you shall see again
no more forever. The LORD will fight for you, and you shall
hold your peace." And the LORD said to Moses, "Why do you cry
to Me? Tell the children of Israel to go forward. But lift up your
rod, and stretch out your hand over the sea and divide it. And the
children of Israel shall go on dry ground through the midst of the
sea. And I indeed will harden the hearts of the Egyptians, and
they shall follow them. So I will gain honor over Pharaoh and
over all his army, his chariots, and his horsemen. Then the
Egyptians shall know that I am the LORD, when I have gained
honor for Myself over Pharaoh, his chariots, and his horsemen."
EXODUS 14:13–18 NKJV

God responds to His people and instructs Moses to use
what he has been given (God's power) to overcome the
fear and move forward in God's promise. God let Moses
know that the people did not need to cry out to Him in
despair (rooted in fear) for He had already given them
what they needed to address this situation.

I do not believe God had an issue with Moses crying
out to Him. It appears that God's concern was with the
motivation behind the cry. There was no need to cry out
in despair because God had already revealed His will
for His people to be set free. God's question to Moses,
Why do you cry to Me?, required that Moses as the
leader of God's people be aware of his motivation for

seeking God. Was Moses crying out from a place of despair like the people? Or was he crying out as a leader of God's people seeking divine strategy for the situation that was before him?

God in His lovingkindness, answered the cry of His people with detailed instructions as to how he would bring them through this situation. God's ways are truly amazing! Don't hesitate to praise as you learn His ways. Days 4–29 encourages you to experience God's ways as you explore common areas of life where fear can take hold.

Part III
As You Learn His Ways, Sing Your Song!

Then Moses and the children of Israel sang this song to the LORD, and spoke, saying: "I will sing to the LORD, For He has triumphed gloriously! The horse and its rider He has thrown into the sea! The LORD is my strength and song, And He has become my salvation; He is my God, and I will praise Him; My father's God, and I will exalt Him."
EXODUS 15:1–2 NKJV

When the Israelites saw the great power of God, how He delivered them from Pharaoh's army, they praised Him in song. Their hearts were overcome with joy and the lyrics flowed from their souls, right there on the seashore. On Day 30, you are exhorted to discover your song of deliverance. God delights in your praise. He inhabits your praise. Embrace it. Celebrate it. Don't stop praising Him on Day 30; praise Him for the rest of your days!

PART I

When Fear Speaks,
Cry Out to God!

PRAYER

Dear God,

Your word says that you have "come that I might have life and have it more abundantly."[2] Please hear the cry of my heart. I need a change in my life. I realize that there is a deep desire in me to do more, to be more, to reach my full potential in you, to experience the abundance that you have promised me in your word. Something has hindered me from doing this and I believe that "something" is fear. I can no longer accept a mediocre existence. My prayer is to walk in deliverance, starting here and starting now. Please use this book to speak to my heart that I might walk in liberty and "press toward the mark for the prize of the high calling"[3] I have in Christ Jesus. It is in Your name that I pray, Amen.

CONTRARY WINDS

*And he saw them toiling in rowing; for the wind was contrary
unto them: and about the fourth watch of the night he cometh
unto them, walking upon the sea, and would have passed by
them. But when they saw him walking upon the sea, they
supposed it had been a spirit, and cried out: For they all saw
him, and were troubled. And immediately he talked with them,
and saith unto them, Be of good cheer: it is I; be not afraid.*
MARK 6:48–50 KJV

As I sit on the beach searching for answers,
He speaks.
My Love, the answer is simple. It's a choice.
It's your choice.
See the birds? There are those that soar high above
the water and some that soar low. There are those
that rest on the water and go with the flow.
There are others that nurse the shoreline finding
comfort there. But, as soon as the waves rush in
they scurry to land that's clear.
And look at him walking along the sand
not concerned about the waves or a single man.
He stops to rest and stretch his wings not focusing on
the others in search of the finer things.

For they battle to the forefront where they know
their food is sure but somehow this little guy thinks
less is actually more.
And who's to say at any time you won't be all of
them. The importance is the motivation.
What guides you to your end?
Some take risks and some like to play it safe.
What road in life will lead you to that place?
Of wholeness, of comfort, of joy and release.
Of desire, of passion, of self-identity and peace.
As I watched the parasailer I began to understand
What keeps me locked here, and not in the place of
this man, is FEAR.
False **E**vidence **A**ppearing **R**eal![4] How long will you
allow it to steal your abundant life?

— LeSette M. Wright © 2003

This book begins with a challenge. A challenge to en-vision yourself in the lines of the poem above. Imagine sitting on the beach, the morning dew fallen freshly on your cheeks. Watching the sun rise and reflecting on your life: the joys, the struggles, every person you have been blessed to meet, every experience you have encountered.

You reflect and ask God for direction. Your heart's desire is to not waste the cherished life you have been given. You pause in the preciousness of this moment and thank God for bringing you to this place. You thank Him for allowing you to see the sun rise and feel it's warmth on your skin, overcome with the beauty of the ocean as the waves crash upon the shore, in awe of each seagull as they soar on the wind and relax on the water.

As your eyes scan this beautiful work of art you notice a lone parasailor. He relaxes on the wind, suspended in midair above the ocean. You think to yourself, "Wow, what courage!" And then it happens, the gentle voice of God meets you there. He speaks to you and you are forever changed. The lover of your soul poetically embraces you with His words. He allows you to know that He has been with you and listening to every meditation of your heart.

The Creator uses creation to teach you a lesson that you must learn in order to move forward in His purpose for your life. He shares the above poem with you. He tells you that the parasailor can soar high because the wind is contrary unto him. He reminds you of the winds that have raged through your life: loss of loved ones, times of unsurety, and situations that have rocked the very foundation of your being. He reminds you of the overwhelming sense of fear that consumed you during those times.

While you thought you would never make it through these situations, you did. Not only did you survive, you overcame! Yes, you indeed made it through those contrary winds. And even though those past victories are real, you continue to find yourself stuck in many areas. You want the abundant life, but somehow you struggle to grasp it. Something continues to hinder you. Could that something be fear?

Point to Ponder

Contrary winds come not to destroy you but to strengthen you.

Prayer for Power

Dear God, help me to know the areas in my life where fear has been crippling me. Change my perspective that I might see Your blessings in the storms of life and not fear the raging winds. I ask this in Jesus name, Amen.

Pursue your Purpose

"God knows the plans He has for you. They are plans to prosper you and not harm you. They are plans to give you a hope and a future."[5] Take some time today to meditate in this truth. Write out the scriptural passage in Jeremiah 29:11 on the top of a sheet of paper. After you have written the passage, list three hopes you have for your future. Commit these hopes in prayer to God, and ask for clarity of vision, strategy and purpose. Walk by faith in pursuit of your purpose, commanding fear to release its grasp and holding fast to "the peace of God which surpasses all understanding."[6]

FACE IT TO ERASE IT

But the LORD said to Moses, "Do not fear him, for I have given him into your hand, and all his people and his land; and you shall do to him as you did to Sihon, king of the Amorites, who lived at Heshbon."

NUMBERS 21:34–35 NKJV

Have you ever noticed how often the command, "Do not fear" appears in scripture? It appears quite frequently. We might deduce from this that humankind is prone to fear. In the scripture above, Moses is instructed not to fear King Og. This is the same Moses that God used to part the Red Sea and lead the Israelites through on dry land. For Moses, after a victory like that, fear is still an issue? Yes, it is!

With each new battle God looks at the heart of His people and if He identifies fear, God requires them to face it. Moses did not say, "God, I'm afraid of King Og." But God is clearly aware that this is the case. If there is fear in your life you must face it to erase it! God will nullify the effect or force of fear as we confront it in our lives. Has God given you victory upon victory, yet you continue to fear in the same and/ or different areas of your life?

Point to Ponder

When you face your fears, you will experience the God-given power, to overcome them. You must face it to erase it!

Prayer for Power

Dear God, there are areas in my life where you have given me victory upon victory, yet I continue to fear. Give me the discernment and understanding to face these fears that you might erase them, and I might walk in Your "power, love and a sound mind."[7] I ask this in the powerful name of Jesus the Christ, Amen.

Pursue your Purpose

Yesterday you wrote down three hopes that you have for your future. Today, revisit those three hopes. What are the fears you have regarding these hopes? List these fears on a sheet of paper. It may also be helpful to ask a close friend, spouse, or family member about their perceptions of any fears you may have in these areas. Sometimes our fears are not obvious to us; God may reveal them to us through the counsel of others. As these fears become clear through prayer and counsel, you will face them to erase them!

ABASE IT TO REPLACE IT

So when the woman saw that the tree was good for food, that it was pleasant to the eyes, and a tree desirable to make one wise, she took of its fruit and ate. She also gave to her husband with her, and he ate. Then the eyes of both of them were opened, and they knew that they were naked; and they sewed fig leaves together and made themselves coverings. And they heard the sound of the LORD God walking in the garden in the cool of the day, and Adam and his wife hid themselves from the presence of the LORD God among the trees of the garden. Then the LORD God called to Adam and said to him, "Where are you?" So he said, "I heard Your voice in the garden, and I was afraid because I was naked; and I hid myself."

GENESIS 3:6–10 NKJV

Why is fear such an issue for humankind? After Adam and Eve ate from the tree of the knowledge of good and evil, fear became an issue. In Genesis 3 we find Adam and Eve attempting to hide from God because of fear. Adam says, "I heard Your voice in the garden, and I was afraid because I was naked; and I hid myself."[8]

Placing the voice of Satan above the voice of God will always open the door for fear to enter, leaving you naked and trying to hide. God instructed Adam and Eve to not eat from the tree of the knowledge of good and evil. When they decided to do this anyway, they raised their knowledge and the knowledge of the serpent above the knowledge of God. When we abase something, we bring it low, as in to lower in rank. In order to overcome fear and walk in God's purpose for your life, you must abase everything that exalts itself above the "knowledge of God."[9] God's word must have the pre-eminence.

Point to Ponder

Giving God's voice the pre-eminence closes the door to fear.

Prayer for Power

Lord, help me today to abase every voice that exalts itself above the knowledge of God and replace those dissenting voices with Your word. "I can do all things through Christ who strengthens me". Lead me as I strive to walk in the fullness of your abundant life. In Jesus' name, Amen.

Pursue your Purpose

Becoming aware of the fears that hinder you from walking fully in your abundant life requires that you acknowledge the "power of voice" that you have given them. These fears have had success because you have allowed the voice of fear to be exalted over the voice of God. Take some time to meditate on how the voice of fear has been speaking in each area of your life. For example, if fear says, "You will never be able to start your own business," abase that voice and replace it with God's word: "I can do all things through Christ who strengthens me."[10] Practice this skill for each area of your life where fear has been speaking. You will develop your ability to exalt God's voice over the voice of fear as you continue with this practice.

PART II

As God Answers, Learn His Ways!

FEAR OF LOVE

And we have known and believed the love that God hath to us.
God is love: and he that dwelleth in love dwelleth in God, and
God in him.
1 JOHN 4:12

God loves you so much, in innumerable ways.
Sixty-six books set the stage
of a trinity love affair with humanity.
God's love is good, come taste and see!

— LeSette M. Wright © 2018

The Bible is the greatest love story ever told. And when you think about it, this actually makes sense. Why? Because, God is love. God defines love. God emits love. If you look up love in the dictionary you should see a picture of God; the all-sufficient one. Yes, love is truly all you need. However, I doubt that the Beatles understood the theological depth of the lyrics when their song was written. They were really saying all you need is God.

God's love is unfathomable. The more God loves me the more I question my ability to love as God does. I've even tried to force God to give up on me, but God's love is so stubborn all He says is I'll "never leave you nor forsake you."[11]

I'm ashamed to admit it but sometimes I have a hard time receiving God's love. It makes me uncomfortable. It makes me change my ways. It makes me forget about self. This love is not to be feared as in **F**alse **E**vidence **A**ppearing **R**eal. There is nothing false about God's love. God's love is to be feared as in honored, reverenced, and worshiped. "For God so loved the world that he gave his only begotten son, that whosoever believes in him would not perish but have everlasting life."[12]

Point to Ponder

God is love. Love renders fear impotent. When we accept Jesus Christ as our Lord and Savior, love comes to indwell us.

Prayer for Power

God of love, thank you for rendering fear impotent. Help me walk in your overcoming power and love this day and every day. If I become afraid of Your love, may that fear turn to reverence and worship that I may honor Your love for me and all of creation. In Jesus' name, Amen.

Pursue your Purpose

It is God's love that renders fear powerless and propels you into your abundant life. The more you embrace God's love, the power therein, and its ability to work in and through you, the more comfort you will have with your purpose and confidence to walk in it.

Does the perfect love of God intimidate you? If this is the case, acknowledge it and release it. God loves you so deeply and profoundly. You were created in God's image and likeness to prosper. God wants you to reverence Him but never to be afraid of Him. Fearless pursuit of your purpose requires that you embrace this truth.

NO FEAR IN LOVE

There is no fear in love; but perfect love casteth out fear; because fear hath torment. **He that feareth is not made perfect in love.**[13]

1 JOHN 4:18 KJV

God is love. If we restate the above passage, it could read: "There is no fear in God; but (the) perfect God casteth out fear; because fear hath torment. The one who fears is not made perfect in God." Opening your heart to God's deep and abiding love requires vulnerability. Either you will be vulnerable to Satan's fear or God's love. The choice is yours. You can never pursue the fullness of your purpose without embracing God's love and getting rid of fear. Fear will torment you if you allow it to. Some are so tormented by fear that they look for relief in alcohol, drugs, and other means, only to find that the fear remains. Torment is fear-dependent. Love is an act of the will. Perfect love is the prescription for fear.

Point to Ponder

Perfect love is the prescription for fear. What prescriptions have you used to deal with fear in your life?

Prayer for Power

Merciful God, in You I find perfect love. May I permit Your perfect love to cast fear out of my life. Help me each and every day to choose the way of love and not the way of fear. May the power of Your Holy Spirit fill me afresh this day so that I may move forward in Your purpose for my life with a sound mind and the blessed assurance that You will "perfect the things that concern me."[14] In Jesus' name, Amen.

Pursue your Purpose

As perfect love casts fear out of your life, what have you been called to accomplish this day, tomorrow, and in the future? Every day that we are alive, God has a purpose and a plan for us. Remember to not be so future-focused that you miss what God is doing in your life today. Perhaps today there is someone whom you are to encourage, a need you have the ability to supply, or a system you are called to impact. God has given you an assignment that is specifically yours to fulfill. Don't allow fear to block you.

Pursue your purpose and celebrate abundant life.

LOVE NEVER FAILS

Love is patient, love is kind and is not jealous; love does not brag and is not arrogant, does not act unbecomingly; it does not seek its own, is not provoked, does not take into account a wrong suffered, does not rejoice in unrighteousness, but rejoices with the truth; bears all things, believes all things, hopes all things, endures all things. Love never fails.
1 CORINTHIANS 13:4–8a

What does love look like? Try to picture it in your mind's eye. Now, picture fear. The difference is drastic. 1 Corinthians 13 provides a beautiful description of God's love. This is the love that never fails. This love stands firm, looks fear in the eye and commands it to vacate the premises. As a child of God, you are equipped with the love that never fails. It is this love that will walk with you, stand with you. and encourage you in the pursuit of your purpose. Yes, love never fails and neither will you as you conquer fear and walk in the abundant life.

Point to Ponder

Love will always stand. Fear causes us to cower. Stand firm today in love to overcome the stifling effects of fear.

Prayer for Power

Loving God, help me to embody Your patient, kind love. Your perfect love that casts out fear and never fails. As I move forward today in love, strengthen me to stand firm, embracing my journey and walking confidently into the abundant life. This I pray in Your powerful, fearless, loving name, Amen.

Pursue your Purpose

The Greek word for "fails" in 1 Corinthians 13 connotes "falling down." The love that propels us into abundant life in Christ never falls down. As we journey, we may find ourselves stumbling and maybe even falling along the way. It is love that lifts us up, embraces us, and enables us to stand firm in the face of fear. Have you stumbled in your journey and now fear the pursuit of your purpose? Move forward. Love will keep you. Love will help you stand!

FEAR OF DEATH

Set your mind on things above, not on things on the earth. For you died, and your life is hidden with Christ in God.
COLOSSIANS 3:2–3

Do you fear death? Or, perhaps dying without fulfilling your purpose or doing the things that you wanted to do? Many people have a "bucket list" of things they want to do before they "kick the bucket." Kicking the bucket has a negative connotation. As Christians, we do not view death negatively. We understand that Christ conquered death and the grave (1 Corinthians 15:55–56). For the Christian, death is a passing from life on earth to eternal life with Christ. So, I prefer to call my list of accomplishments before leaving earth my "glory list," things to do before I go to glory.

Fear of death can hinder us from achieving our glory list and walking in our purpose in Christ Jesus. As Christians, we know that "death" is required in order for us to walk in our abundant life in Christ. Every day we are called to "die to self." Colossians 3:2–3 instructs us to "set our minds on things above" knowing that "we died and our lives our hidden with Christ in God." Setting our minds on things above is an important strategy for us to overcome fear. Our minds are the battlefield. The things we set our minds on can either strengthen or hinder our harmony with the divine. Acknowledging that our lives are hidden with Christ in God allows our glory list to be crafted by our Creator.

Point to Ponder

There is no room for fear of death in your life. You died, and your life is hidden with Christ in God.

Prayer for Power

Victorious God, You conquered death, hell, and the grave, therefore, I am more than a conqueror through You. Help me to walk in this truth allowing You to craft my glory list. This I ask in Your most precious, holy name, Amen.

Pursue your Purpose

Has the fear of death hindered you from walking in your abundant life in Christ? Practicing the skill of "setting your mind on things above"[15] will help you pursue your purpose without fear. Meditating on, practicing, and reciting Philippians 4:4–8 will strengthen you in this area.

YOU WERE DEAD

And you were dead in your trespasses and sins, in which you formerly walked according to the course of this world, according to the prince of the power of the air, of the spirit that is now working in the sons of disobedience. Among them we too all formerly lived in the lusts of our flesh, indulging the desires of the flesh and of the mind, and were by nature children of wrath, even as the rest. But God, being rich in mercy, because of His great love with which He loved us, even when we were dead in our transgressions, made us alive together with Christ (by grace you have been saved), and raised us up with Him, and seated us with Him in the heavenly places in Christ Jesus, so that in the ages to come He might show the surpassing riches of His grace in kindness toward us in Christ Jesus. For by grace you have been saved through faith; and not of yourselves, it is the gift of God; not as a result of works, so that no one may boast. For we are His workmanship, created in Christ Jesus for good works, which God prepared beforehand so that we would walk in them.

EPHESIANS 2:1–10

You were dead in your sins but by God's grace through Christ Jesus you have been saved. Because of this gift of God, you have no reason to fear anything. God has prepared good works for you to walk in and as a matter of fact you were created for this purpose. The Creator has fashioned you to bring glory to Himself as you walk in your abundant life in Christ Jesus. So, why fear death? Dying to sin and dying to self are necessary steps of our journey. It is through that dying that we actually live. By God's grace through faith in Christ Jesus we have God's unmerited favor. God has prepared good works in advance for us to walk in. All we have to do is walk in them; however, fear comes to hinder that process. Don't allow that to happen. Through Christ Jesus, you have the victory over fear.

Point to Ponder

"You are God's workmanship, created in Christ Jesus for good works, which God prepared beforehand so that you would walk in them."[16] From death to life, God has ordered your steps. Don't allow fear to detour you.

Prayer for Power

All powerful God, You have saved me from death and given me new life in Christ. Thank You for creating me for good works which You have prepared in advance for me to walk in. Strengthen me to walk in victory, denounce fear, and glorify You with my life. In Jesus' name, Amen.

Pursue your Purpose

You were dead in sin. You are now alive in Christ. On this day, how will you denounce fear and walk in a manner that is reflective of new life in Christ?

FROM DEATH TO LIFE

One day I woke up and realized I died.
Became aware of the deception and lies
that kept me tied to an idea of me.
How I was and how I needed to be.
I became aware that I was no longer free
to do what I see as reality.
Had to set my mind on things above
'cause new life with Christ
meant I had been bought with a price.
And I had been a Christian for years.
Had cast all my cares on God.
Walking with my feet shod with the gospel
of the preparation of peace.
Watching God open minds
that had been blinded by the beast.
And all the while never realized
I had been holding on to that childish me,
the one that encouraged me to behave selfishly,
causing my conversations with the most high
to contain words like me, myself, and I.
Then one day something snapped
and I internalized the fact that I was dead.
Thoughts of me as the priority
no longer running through my head.
I was living for the Savior. This was major.

Generational sin that once kept me
shucking and jiving and dipping and diving
my calling was severed.
The enemy could no longer use that
as leverage against me of why I could not be
the way God had destined me.
One day I woke up and realized I died
and my soul cried Halleluiah.
'Cause I understood that it was only then
that I was free to be alive!

— LeSette M. Wright © 2003

From death to life is a journey; a journey filled with bright places and dark places. From death to life. Whether we cry from an airconditioned living room in the United States or from the bush in war-torn Africa, God hears us. He hears the condition and attitude of each heart. He hears our brokenness and responds. God knows that we will be set free and delivered when we release the burden that we have carried in denial. Often kidding ourselves, saying we have laid the burden at His feet but still functioning in fear. Fear of God's providence. Fear of trusting Him with our very lives. Fear of God disappointing us like others have done. And then in the midst of the storm, God allows a phone call from a friend. He sends a bird to your window with a song. He allows a rainbow to fill the sky. He leads you to that scripture that speaks exactly to where you are. God meets us at the end of ourselves. Because that's where He needed us to be so that we could face the reality of our condition and give Him the glory that is due His name. God reminds us once again that it's not about us. The plan is so much bigger. He reminds us that dying can be very uncomfortable. But He calls us to die to self on a daily basis. God reminds us that He is in control and fear is forced to flee in the face of a renewed faith in Him.

Point to Ponder

From death to life, fear is conquered. Fall in love with the process.

Prayer for Power

Most gracious God, as I journey from death to life, help me fall in love with the process. Empower me by Your Holy Spirit to walk by faith and embrace life abundantly. In Jesus' name, Amen.

Pursue your Purpose

Have you embraced the journey from death to life? Walking in life more abundantly requires that we fall in love with the process. How will you overcome fear today and honor your process of abundant life in Christ?

FEAR OF CHANGE

I urge you therefore, brethren, by the mercies of God, to present your bodies a living and holy sacrifice, acceptable to God, which is your spiritual service of worship, And do not be conformed to this world but be transformed by the renewing of your mind, that you may prove what the will of God is, that which is good and acceptable and perfect.

ROMANS 12:1–2

Change is a mandatory component of the Christian's life. We are instructed to not change our character and mindset to conform to the common way or worldly way of life, but to be transformed. The Greek word used here for *transform* is where we get the English word *metamorphosis*. Think of the beautiful butterfly that used to be a caterpillar. This is akin to the radical transformation that we are called to undergo as Christians. We are transformed by the renewing of our minds. The old mind that used to entertain fear must go and the new mind must emerge. The Christian must not fear change in Christ Jesus but embrace it. This is the only way to walk in the "good, acceptable, and perfect will of God."[17] This is our abundant life.

Point to Ponder

Being transformed by the renewing of your mind requires an extreme makeover.

Prayer for Power

Dear Lord, I thank You for calling me to undergo an extreme makeover in You. Help me put off my former way of life and put on newness of life in You. Strengthen me as I undergo transformation. As the butterfly struggles with the cocoon and ultimately breaks free, may my wings be strengthened to fly into my purpose and break free from the fear that has bound me. This I ask in Your most precious and Holy name, Amen.

Pursue your Purpose

How does your thinking and character reflect your journey in Christ? Do you think and act the same way you did when you first believed? What role has fear played in hindering your transformative process? Meditating in and practicing Ephesians 4:17–32 will aid you as you journey in your abundant life.

CONFORMED TO THE IMAGE

And we know that God causes all things to work together for good to those who love God, to those who are called according to His purpose. For those whom He foreknew, He also predestined to become conformed to the image of His Son, so that He would be the firstborn among many brethren; and these whom He predestined, He also called; and these whom He called, He also justified; and these whom He justified, He also glorified. What then shall we say to these things? If God is for us, who is against us? He who did not spare His own Son, but delivered Him over for us all, how will He not also with Him freely give us all things? Who will bring a charge against God's elect? God is the one who justifies; who is the one who condemns? Christ Jesus is He who died, yes, rather who was raised, who is at the right hand of God, who also intercedes for us. Who will separate us from the love of Christ? Will tribulation, or distress, or persecution, or famine, or nakedness, or peril, or sword? Just as it is written,

"For Your sake we are being put to death all day long; We were considered as sheep to be slaughtered."

But in all these things we overwhelmingly conquer through Him who loved us. For I am convinced that neither death, nor life, nor angels, nor principalities, nor things present, nor things to come, nor powers, nor height, nor depth, nor any other created thing, will be able to separate us from the love of God, which is in Christ Jesus our Lord.

ROMANS 8:28–39

You were predestined to be conformed to the image of Christ Jesus. Given that this is the reality, one might think that the journey would be a simple one. This could not be farther from the truth. The process of changing from the old self to the new self has great challenges. As the old mind and character die and the new mind and character emerge, the difficulties nurture the journey. God causes all these things to work together for good. These things will not all be good, but they sure will produce good in the end. That "good" is the manifestation of the mind and character of Christ in and through us. The Romans 8 passage so beautifully lays out the abundant life journey. First, we are predestined, then called, then justified, then glorified. Fear tries to inject itself into this process to hinder it. Don't fear the change God is facilitating in your life. Walk with God knowing that His promise is to "prosper you and not harm you, to give you a hope and a future."[18]

Point to Ponder

The process of conforming you to the image of Christ Jesus means you are predestined, called, justified, and glorified.

Prayer for Power

Omnipotent God, I stand in awe of Your transforming power. When the road gets rough, help me to remember that You cause all things to "work together for good for them that love You and are the called according to Your purpose."[19] Help me build memorials lest I forget that Your grace is sufficient and Your love never fails. In Jesus' name, I pray, Amen.

Pursue your Purpose

When Jesus went through the process of transfiguration on the mountain (Matthew 17:2), He instructed the disciples to fear not. The Greek word for *transfigured* in Matthew 17 is the same Greek word used for *transformed* in Romans 12:1–2. This speaks of a total metamorphosis. As we undergo a transformation of mind and character, this might prove to be scary for those watching our lives. Don't allow this fearfulness to distract you from your purpose. Stay focused and pray that God will open the eyes of their understanding, that they may see Him at work in your life, as well as theirs.

THE HEART OF A ROSE

Have you ever seen the heart of a rose? Over the years, I've received roses many times. On each occasion, I placed these beautiful creations of God in a vase and arranged them just so. I smelled them and glanced to admire their beauty several times a day. I encouraged visitors to respect and admire their presence.

Each time I received these precious flowers, I wanted to learn to love them better, to care for them in a way that would extend their life. I remember how I learned to nurture my roses. I placed them in luke-warm water, keeping the foliage from touching the water. I listened to different ideas like adding sugar or lemon to the water. I also tried the packets of fresh flower food that came with my arrangements.

But never did I see the heart of a rose, until the special day when the many layers of petals opened. I was privileged to see their hearts and the site was breathtaking. I realized that I had never seen the depth of their beauty until that moment. As a matter of fact, I realized that I had never truly seen a rose until I saw its heart.

I reflect on a trip I once took to Mexico. I purchased a dress in the *mercado* (market) and asked an artist there to paint roses on the dress. When I returned to pick up the dress, I was surprised. The painted flowers did not look anything like the roses I had seen in my lifetime. They were pretty but not what I expected. I took the dress home and while I loved it there was still a piece of me that wished the roses looked like my mental picture of them.

Well, now I realize that this artist had already seen that the true beauty of a rose involved seeing its heart. The roses on my dress were opened to reveal their hearts. Since I had never before seen the heart of a rose, I could not recognize its true essence, its true beauty, its true life. But, now I could. And I thought, what if I never had the chance to see the heart of a rose? I realized my life would have been cheated.

As I admired this bouquet of roses that had revealed their hearts to me, I could not help but notice the few that hadn't. Do they need more time? Will they ever open up? Then I realized that these were once the only roses I had known. Their's the only beauty I had known. And now that I saw what they were destined to be, I wanted them all to bloom to the fullest. But, I realized that even if they didn't they were still beautiful. I knew I could not let their beauty disappear in the face of the rose that bloomed to reveal its heart. I knew that I could never look at roses in the same manner. While I would always admire their beauty, I would always see their potential to be more. To show the world who they really are. And as each beautiful bouquet of roses began to bow their heads never to look up again, I noticed the ones that lived the longest were the roses that had revealed their hearts. Those that dared to show the world who they really were. These roses had lived an abundant life.

Point to Ponder

Being conformed to the image of Christ Jesus requires change. Change requires vulnerability. Vulnerability requires transparency. Transparency reveals our hearts.

Prayer for Power

Omniscient God, Rose of Sharon, it is You who nurtures me to wholeness and cultivates Your character to shine forth through me. Help me God to not fear the vulnerability and transparency that transformation requires. "Search my heart and know me. Remove everything from me that is contrary to Your will and lead me in Your way everlasting."[20] This I pray in Jesus' name, Amen.

Pursue your Purpose

How are the roses in the story reflective of your transformative journey in Christ? Do you have a fear of being vulnerable and/or transparent with God? With others? With self?

FEAR OF THE ENEMY

Be of sober spirit, be on the alert. Your adversary, the devil,
prowls about like a roaring lion, seeking someone to devour, But
resist him, firm in your faith, knowing that the same experiences
of suffering are being accomplished by your brethren who are in
the world. And after you have suffered for a little while, the God
of all grace, who called you to His eternal glory in Christ, will
Himself perfect, confirm, strengthen and establish you.

1 PETER 5:8–10

So often we find ourselves intimidated by Satan. We have gone as far as to create a physical form of what we think he looks like: a human form with red skin, a red suit, long tail, horns, and a pitchfork. Most assuredly Satan does not show up like this in our daily experience. The aforementioned scripture likens Satan to a roaring lion, roaming and seeking someone to devour. Satan is always on the job. He does not call in sick or make excuses for why he could not work towards his mission on any given day.

So, if Satan is always on the job, what about the Christian? Are we as committed and persistent in our mission? Or are we allowing a spirit of fear and intimidation to hinder our journey?

As Christians, we should not fear the enemy. If you have felt the Spirit of God prompting you to do something that you have not done, the time is now. Do not wait any longer. Don't be responsible for telling your abundant life to go to hell. Because that's exactly what you are doing when you fear the enemy and do not respond to God's promptings. We all experience trials, suffering, and challenges. These times are opportunities for us to encourage one another in the family of God. Satan may try his best to wreak havoc in our lives, but our God has promised to perfect, confirm, strengthen, and establish us.[21]

Point to Ponder

Suffering plays a role in conforming us to the image of Christ Jesus.

Prayer for Power

God of peace, when the storms of life are raging, fill me with Your joy. I thank You that nothing is wasted as You perfect, confirm, strengthen, and establish me. May I never fear the enemy, understanding that You have already overcome him and I am "more than a conqueror"[22] through You. In Jesus' name, Amen.

Pursue your Purpose

Satan may be the source of some suffering in our lives, but God allows that suffering to build His character in us. Have you allowed fear of the enemy to hinder your abundant life in Christ?

AS I WAS WITH MOSES

Moses my servant is dead, Now then, you and all these people, get ready to cross the Jordan river into the land I am about to give them – to the Israelites. I will give you every place where you set your foot, as I promised Moses. No one will be able to stand up against you all the days of your life. As I was with Moses, so I will be with you; I will never leave you nor forsake you.

JOSHUA 1:2,3,5

As the book of Joshua opens, Moses is dead and God has commanded Joshua to lead the people across the Jordan into the promised land. God gives Joshua a "pep talk" if you will. God's pep talk with Joshua is a notification that He is no respecter of persons. He wants Joshua to know that it's not about him and it's not about Moses but it's about a promise that He made to his people. God instructs Joshua, "as I was with Moses, so shall I be with you."[23] If you are going to overcome fear of the enemy you must realize that it's not about you. Your walking in the abundant life is about a God who is determined to fulfill His promises. "The God who has called you is faithful, and He will bring it to pass."[24]

Point to Ponder

God has promised to never leave you or forsake you.[25]

Prayer for Power

God of Love, I thank you that You are "no respecter of persons."[26] Your promise to all of your children is to never leave us or forsake us. Help me to hide this truth in my heart and walk in the joy of knowing that You are a Faithful God, and You will bring every promise to pass. In Jesus' name, Amen.

Pursue your Purpose

What is God calling you to do that you have not done? What enemy in your life do you need to conquer? God wants you to succeed. You are "more than a conqueror in Christ Jesus."[27] God loves you so much that He has left you a pep talk called the Bible. The Bible contains the wisdom and encouragement you need to overcome the enemy. Write the plan. Plan the work. Work the plan.

BE STRONG AND COURAGEOUS

*Be strong and courageous, because you will lead these people to
inherit the land I swore to their forefathers to give them. Be
strong and very courageous because you will lead these people to
inherit the land I swore to their forefathers to give them. Be
strong and very courageous. Be careful to obey all the law my
servant Moses gave you: do not turn from it to the right or to the
left, that you may be successful wherever you go. Do not let this
Book of the Law depart from your mouth; meditate on it day and
night, so that you may be careful to do everything written in it.
Then you will be prosperous and successful.*

JOSHUA 1:6–8

The book of Joshua provides a blueprint for overcoming
fear and defeat. God advises Joshua several times to be
strong and courageous. God in His omniscience is
aware of the enemy's tactics. He advises Joshua to
combat a spirit of fear. "Have I not commanded you?
Be strong and courageous. Do not be terrified. Do not
be discouraged, for the Lord your God will be with you
wherever you go."[28] Joshua is exhorted with the surety
that God is with him. The presence of the omnipotent
God is our blessed assurance against the enemy.

Point to Ponder

Be strong and courageous. God is with you wherever you go.

Prayer for Power

Gracious God, may I hide Your word in my heart that I might not sin against it.[29] May I meditate in Your word day and night that my way would be prosperous and I would have good success.[30] May I recognize the blessings You have placed in my path, knowing that while man looks at the outward, You look at the heart.[31] In Jesus' name, I pray, Amen.

Pursue your Purpose

Sometimes the path to our abundant life includes unexpected allies. Read and meditate on the role of Rahab in Joshua 2. Are there people around you who God may want to use as unexpected allies? Don't miss your blessing because of the way in which it is packaged.

FEAR OF THE FIGHT

Finally, be strong in the Lord, and in the strength of His might.
Put on the full armor of God that you may be able to stand firm
against the schemes of the evil one. For our struggle is not
against flesh and blood, but against the rulers, against the
powers, against the world forces of this darkness, against the
spiritual forces of wickedness in the heavenly places.
EPHESIANS 6:10–12

There is a spiritual dynamic to every battle. Ephesians 6 tells us that our struggle is not against flesh and blood. The Greek word for *struggle* in this text can also be translated as *wrestle* or *fight*. As believers in Jesus Christ, we must not fear the fight. We must however understand that the weapons we fight with are not worldly. Our weapons are "mighty through God for the pulling down of strongholds."[32] God has given us a full armor to "resist the devil and stand firm in our identity in Christ."[33] So, don't fear the fight. Dress daily in your armor and be strong in the Lord and in His mighty power.

Point to Ponder

Your struggle is not against flesh and blood.

Prayer for Power

Dear God, I thank You for wisdom in warfare. May my feet remain shod with the preparation of the gospel of peace. May I take up the shield of faith, the helmet of salvation, and the sword of the spirit. May the belt of truth enfold me and the breastplate of righteousness keep me as I seek You with all prayer and petition, praying in the Spirit always.[34] In Jesus' name, Amen.

Pursue your Purpose

Spiritual warfare is a central component of the believer's life. As you pursue God's purpose for your life, the enemy will try to stop you by any means possible. If you don't already have a prayer partner or prayer team, invite an individual and/or group to commit to praying for your journey and supporting you in the battle. Allow the Spirit of God to lead you to the person/people he has appointed to stand with you in prayer.

COMMANDER-IN-CHIEF

*Then they told David, saying, "Look, the Philistines are fighting
against Keilah, and they are robbing the threshing floors."
Therefore David inquired of the Lord, saying, "Shall I go and
attack these Philistines?" And the Lord said to David, "Go and
attack the Philistines, and save Keilah." But David's men said
to him, "Look, we are afraid here in Judah. How much more
then if we go to Keilah against the armies of the Philistines?"
Then David inquired of the Lord once again. And the Lord
answered him and said, "Arise, go down to Keilah. For I will
deliver the Philistines into your hand." And David and his men
went to Keilah and fought with the Philistines, struck them with
a mighty blow, and took away their livestock. So David saved the
inhabitants of Keilah. Now it happened, when Abiathar the son
of Ahimelech fled to David at Keilah, that he went down with
an ephod in his hand. And Saul was told that David had gone to
Keilah. So Saul said, "God has delivered him into my hand, for
he has shut himself in by entering a town that has gates and
bars." Then Saul called all the people together for war, to go
down to Keilah to besiege David and his men. When David knew
that Saul plotted evil against him, he said to Abiathar the
priest, "Bring the ephod here." Then David said, "O Lord God of
Israel, I pray, tell Your servant." And the Lord said, "He will
come down." Then David said, "Will the men of Keilah deliver
me and my men into the hand of Saul?" And the Lord said,
"They will deliver you." So David and his men, about six*

hundred, arose and departed from Keilah and went wherever they could go. Then it was told Saul that David had escaped from Keilah; so he halted the expedition.

1 SAMUEL 23:1–13 NKJV

In 1 Samuel 23, we get a sneak peek into David's relationship with God as Commander-in-Chief. David inquires of the Lord as to whether or not he and his men should fight the Philistines. The Lord instructs him to go. After David received these instructions, he shares them with his men. The men are afraid to go so David goes back to God and inquires again. God confirms the previous instructions, so David and his men go and God gives them the victory.

We also see that David prays to the Lord for instructions as to how to deal with Saul. God reveals that the people of Keilah would hand David over to Saul. David and his men then leave Keilah to prevent this from happening. We see clearly from this passage that David only went to battle as God instructed him to do so. While we must never fear the fight as believers, we must always follow the direction of our Commander-in-Chief.

Point to Ponder

"Trust in the Lord with all your heart, and do not lean on your own understanding. In all your ways acknowledge Him, and He will direct your path."[35]

Prayer for Power

Jehovah Nissi, You are the Lord, my banner. I raise You high over my life, knowing that in You I "live and move and have my being."[36] Thank You for making my path straight. I recognize that the battle belongs to You. Help me to "lean not to my own understanding"[37] and to acknowledge you in all my ways. This I ask in the mighty name of Jesus the Christ, Amen.

Pursue your Purpose

Going to battle without the Lord is a recipe for disaster. Are there battles that you are trying to fight without God's direction? Are you leaning to your own understanding in the pursuit of your purpose?

FALSE SHEPHERDS

The thief comes only to steal and kill, and destroy; I came that
they might have life and might have it abundantly.
JOHN 10:10

The aforementioned John 10 passage is often quoted by
Christians. It is a foundational passage for this
devotional book. So why have I chosen to talk about this
passage under "Fear of the Fight?" There is much
controversy surrounding this text. The context of this
passage is Jesus' discourse presenting Himself as the
Good Shepherd, and false shepherds as the thieves who
come only to steal, kill, and destroy. The foundation of
the abundant life is built upon the acceptance of this
fact.

For the believer, our journey in the way of the
abundant life encounters false shepherds. Shepherds
that selfishly serve to lead us away from Christ instead
of towards Him. Walking in the abundant life entails
accepting Jesus Christ as the way to God and allowing
God to lead us by the power of His Holy Spirit. Do you
see why fear has no place in the hearts and minds of the
Christian? If we cower to the forces that come to turn
us away from God, we surrender our abundant life,

professing with our hearts, minds, and actions that the all-sufficient sacrifice of Christ was impotent.

Point to Ponder

Christ came that you would have life. Live life to the fullest.

Prayer for Power

All powerful God, thank You for sending Christ Jesus so I would have life and live it to the fullest. Help me walk in strength not cowering to the forces of evil, but "having done all to stand."[38] May I stand firm in the full armor that You have given me, not fearing the fight but embracing the journey. This I ask in Your all-sufficient name, Amen.

Pursue your Purpose

You were created for abundant life in Christ Jesus. This abundance life is not defined by material things or monetary riches. It is defined by your relationship with the Good Shepherd. How will you allow this truth to prevail in your life today?

FEAR OF HEIGHTS

Now, behold, the cry of the sons of Israel has come to Me;
furthermore, I have seen the oppression with which the Egyptians
are oppressing them. Therefore, come now and I will send you to
Pharaoh, so that you may bring My people, the sons of Israel,
out of Egypt." But Moses said to God, "Who am I, that I should
go to Pharaoh, and that I should bring the sons of Israel
out of Egypt?
EXODUS 3:9–12

Have you ever watched one of the reality TV shows that challenge people to confront their fear of heights? A person might be required to bungee jump from the roof of a tall building or frantically gather flags while they are spinning in a contraption suspended over the sea.

God has called us to sit in heavenly places. Guess what? That means we cannot be afraid of heights.

When God asked Moses to tell Pharaoh to let His people go, do you remember what happened? Moses began to make excuses for why he could not follow through with this request. Perhaps Moses had gotten comfortable in the desert. He was content functioning behind the scenes. Moses was in hiding after killing an Egyptian. Going to Pharaoh meant he had to face his fear of heights. God was sending him to the highest person in the land to tell him to do something that Moses knew would not be welcomed with open arms. After all, Moses was raised in Pharaoh's house. He knew how things functioned. He knew the intricacies of Pharaoh's lifestyle and the boundaries that existed. He knew that what God was asking him to do was a boundary violation.

Are you ready to violate some boundaries for God? Are you prepared to go when He sends you into the mission field, to follow that ministry vision, to open that business, to enter that marriage? Are you ready to step outside of your comfort zone? Well, this requires taking God out of the box you have put Him in. This requires walking in complete and total dependence on Him. Trusting Him where you can't trace Him; appearing foolish to those who are watching you. This requires you to abandon that fear of heights!

Point to Ponder

You can do all things through Christ who strengthens you![39]

Prayer for Power

King of kings and Lord of lords, thank You for calling me to do great things for the kingdom of God! I trust that with You all things are possible.[40] Help me to use my gifts and talents as You lead me in the narrow way.[41] In Jesus' name, I pray, Amen.

Pursue your Purpose

Has God called you to do something that you feel you are not worthy of? Whether that something is seen as great or lowly in the eyes of mankind, you "can do all things through Christ who strengthens"[42] you. Meditate in Philippians 4:12–13 to see how the Apostle Paul learned this principle in the pursuit of his purpose.

HEAVENLY PLACES

But God, being rich in mercy, because of His great love with
which He loved us, even when we were dead in our
transgressions, made us alive together with Christ (by grace you
have been saved), and raised us up with Him, and seated us with
Him in the heavenly places in Christ Jesus, so that in the ages to
come He might show the surpassing riches of His grace in
kindness toward us in Christ Jesus.

EPHESIANS 2:4–7

God has raised us up with Christ and seated us with Him in heavenly places. By God's grace we walk in a privileged place of favor afforded to us by the all-sufficient sacrifice of our Lord and Savior Jesus Christ. There is nothing we can ever do to earn this positioning. It is granted to us by grace through faith in Jesus. It's not about deservedness as we measure it in our humanity. Have you been hesitant to receive the favor of God in your life because of feeling undeserving? I am thankful that God has not dealt with us as our sins deserve.[43]

Point to Ponder

He has not dealt with us according to our sins, nor rewarded us according to our iniquities. "For as high as the heavens are above the earth, so great is His lovingkindness toward those who fear Him."[44]

Prayer for Power

God of grace and love, you have created me with purpose. Help me to walk in that purpose and break free from the stronghold of deservedness. I am humbled that You have not dealt with me according to my sins. Thank You for salvation through Christ Jesus my Lord. It is in that powerful name that I pray, Amen.

Pursue your Purpose

You were created in the image and likeness of God to bring glory to His name. God has given you a special assignment. God breathed the breath of life into you with purpose, so live your life for Him. Meditate on 1 Corinthians 15:1–11 and break free from the "stronghold of deservedness."[45]

LAUNCH OUT INTO THE DEEP

*When He had finished speaking, He said to Simon, "Launch out
into the deep water and let down your nets for a catch." Simon
answered and said, "Master, we worked hard all night and
caught nothing, but I will do as You say and let down the nets."
When they had done this, they enclosed a great quantity of fish,
and their nets began to break; so they signaled to their partners in
the other boat for them to come and help them. And they came
and filled both of the boats, so that they began to sink.*
LUKE 5:4–7

Have you ever counted the cost of speaking life
to dried bones and evangelizing the lost?
Selah, pause; think on this before you leap
because you have been called
to launch out into the deep.
Let down your nets and get set for a blessing.
Walking by faith and there's no need for guessing
because your strength is found in the Lord's joy
and you know His word can't come back to you void.

Launch out into the deep and let down your nets.
Failing to do so will only lead to regrets.
Stand firm on His Word,
fearfully and wonderfully made.

For no one can lay any other foundation
than the one that has been laid.
Elohim, Jehovah Jireh, El Elyon, El Shaddai.
Jehovah Nissi, the Lord my banner,
start waving Him high.
Keep your eyes on the Lord
walking by faith and not by sight.
Keep your eyes on the Savior
and the Power of His Might.
Launch out into the deep and on the truth.
Please don't sleep because someone needs
to see that Jesus is the key!

— LeSette M. Wright © 1998

The poem above is dedicated to you. God has called you to launch out into the deep. It's time to step away from the shallow places. Fear can no longer be the excuse for you to stay on the shore of life. God has so much more in store for you. If you dare to allow the greatness that is in you to arise, God will B.L.O.W. (Build Love Overflowing with Wonder) your mind.

Point to Ponder

Your miracle is waiting for you in deep waters. Don't let life pass you by. Launch out into the deep.

Prayer for Power

God of abundant love and grace, "teach me to number my days, that I may present to You a heart of wisdom."[46] Confirm the work of my hands and use me for your glory. Strengthen me as I launch out into the deep, leaving behind all dependence on my way and trusting You as my source. In Jesus' name, Amen.

Pursue your Purpose

Life on earth is short. As God teaches you to number your days, celebrate your abundant life and use your time to bring glory to His Name. Meditate in Psalm 90 for support.

FEAR OF THE TRUTH

Lord, I got some stuff to get off of my chest.
I'm trying to be the best at whatever I do.
Constantly seeking you, the Truth.
But it gets tough sometime.
I want to whine and scream and kick
like a spoiled child.
I want to hide in my Daddy's arms for a while.
Sometimes I don't even want to go back
into the game.
I want to stay on the sideline.
I don't even want to be seen.
I want to be invisible; a chameleon blending in
so that I won't be recognized.
Truth be told I want to run, scream, and hide.
Hide from the reality of this existence;
people are dying while the church fights
over trivial nonsense.
This reality is too raw.
I'm all for keeping it real.
But sometimes keeping it real steals my joy!
It's not your will that any should perish.
But yet and still every day we walk around
being average and mediocre Christians.
Scared to open our mouths and witness.
Scared to walk in deliverance.
Scared to be weak in front of our
so-called brothers and sisters.

Why?
Because the truth is they really don't want
to deal with it.
They are dust, fragile, yet still we go on.
We weather the storms.
We refuse to be conformed to this world.
Truth is, this journey ain't easy.

— LeSette M. Wright © 1996

Point to Ponder

The journey in truth requires counting the cost. The road is not always easy but it's worth it. Christ is "the way, the truth, and the life."[47]

Prayer for Power

God of truth and justice, it is Your desire that all should come to the knowledge of the truth. Use me to speak the truth in love as I journey in my purpose. Help me to stand firm in the midst of persecution and to forgive as You have forgiven me. May I always journey in humility and peace. In Jesus' name, Amen.

Pursue your Purpose

Sometimes walking in the truth means you will be rejected by those around you. You must still pursue your purpose in the midst of persecution. May the words of Jesus as recorded in John 8:42–47 encourage you in those challenging times.

TRUTH IS FREEDOM

And you will know the truth and the truth will make you free.
JOHN 8:32

Those whom Christ has set free are free indeed.[48] The Greek word for *free* in John 8:32 means to *make free or exempt from liability*. As children of God, we are exempt from the liability of sin. Through faith in Jesus Christ, this truth propels us in all that we do. Truth is freedom. Functioning in fear is bondage. So, I encourage you to no longer be a slave to fear. We have an insurance policy that has exempted us from liability. Allow this profound truth to dwell in your hearts richly and you will walk in freedom.

Point to Ponder

If the Truth has exempted you from liability, why would you choose to pay the price of a life lived in fear?

Prayer for Power

God of wisdom and truth, enlighten me with the depth of the truth by which I have been set free. Teach me to walk in Your ways and reject the lies of the evil one. Your word is truth, "a lamp upon my feet and a light unto my path."[49] All that is contrary to Your word is that spirit of antichrist which has come into the world to deceive. May my life be a reflection of Your brilliant light which sets the captives free. This I pray in Jesus' name, Amen.

Pursue your Purpose

"I have not written to you because you do not know the truth but because you do know it."[50] Walk in the truth. Meditate in 1 John 2:15–29 for illumination on this truth.

SANCTIFIED IN TRUTH

Sanctify them in the truth; your word is truth.
JOHN 17:17

In John 17, Jesus prayed to the Father on our behalf. He prayed that we would be sanctified in the truth of the word. Jesus asked the Father to set us apart and keep us holy through His word. The power of Jesus' words in prayer resounds throughout the corridors of heaven until this very day. Aren't you glad that Jesus prayed for you? He is seated at the right hand of the Father making intercession even now. The word of God has sanctifying power. Be encouraged in knowing that the word of God sanctifies you in truth as you pursue your purpose.

Point to Ponder

You are holy, equipped for your purpose!

Prayer for Power

Holy God, thank You for sanctifying me in truth. I go forward today delighted to do Your will by the power of the Holy Spirit. I rejoice in knowing that Your word is hidden in my heart, strengthening me for every leg of the race. I yearn for the day when I hear you say, "well done."[51] Until that day, may it be unto me as You have said.[52] In Jesus' name, Amen.

Pursue your Purpose

All the commandments of the Lord are truth. Walk in them. Meditate in Psalm 119:145–152 along the way.

FEAR, YOUR MINISTRY, AND THE END TIMES

There will be signs in sun and moon and stars, and on the earth dismay among nations, in perplexity at the roaring of the sea and the waves, men fainting from fear and the expectation of things which are coming upon the world; for the powers of the heavens will be shaken. Then they will see the Son of Man coming in a cloud with power and great glory. But when these things begin to take place, straighten up and lift up your heads, because your redemption is drawing near.

LUKE 21:25–28

So what does the Bible have to say about fear, your ministry, and the end times? Fear will play a major role in the end times. People will be "fainting from fear and the expectation of things to come."[53] The Greek word translated as *fainting* in Luke 21 does not simply mean *losing heart* it also implies the possibility of expiring. Yes, literally being scared to death!

The picture painted in this text is very troublesome. The effects of fear are grave. But thank God for His exhortation to believers, "But when these things begin to take place, straighten up and lift up your heads, because your redemption is drawing near."[54] We must not allow the spirit of fear to overtake us for we know in whom we trust. End times ministry requires that we remain alert, vigilant, and confident in our God. For if the righteous are scarcely saved, what about the unbeliever?[55] The end times are opportune times to let our light shine for Christ!

Point to Ponder

While others are fainting from fear, you stand strong with uplifted head for your hope is in the Lord!

Prayer for Power

Lord God, thank you for Your words of encouragement regarding the end times and my ministry. Strengthen me to remain steadfast in the midst of crippling fear and horrible circumstances. Help me to reflect Your glory in times of great distress, that people may be delivered from a spirit of fear and fear You in awe and wonder. This I pray in Jesus Name, Amen.

Pursue your Purpose

We are living in the end times. Only God knows when Christ will return. As you wait in joyful hope for the coming of your Savior, may you be steadfast in the pursuit of your purpose.

YOUR MINISTRY

Be on guard, so that your hearts will not be weighted down with dissipation and drunkenness, and the worries of life, and that Day will not come on you suddenly like a trap. For it will come upon all those who dwell on the face of the whole earth. But keep on the alert at all times, praying that you may have strength to escape all these things that are about to take place, and to stand before the Son of Man. Now during the day He was teaching in the temple, but at evening He would go out and spend the night on the mount that is called Olivet. And all the people would get up early in the morning to come to Him in the temple to listen to Him.

LUKE 21:34–38

End times circumstances are so disheartening that Christians are instructed to be on guard against drunken nausea and being consumed with the worries of life. Though we walk by faith and not by sight, we must not think we are exempt from experiencing the stressors of the journey. These words must be taken to heart as we are further cautioned to not let the Day of the Lord come upon us like a trap. Our end times ministry requires that we remain alert and pray without ceasing; pray for strength to stand before the Lord and to escape the things that are to come. As you journey in your purpose, be aware of the impact of circumstances on your spiritual, physical, and mental health. Every day the news is filled with disturbing events. Things that were once considered unfathomable are coming to pass. "In a multitude of counsel there is safety."[56] Gathering with other Christians who can keep you accountable and encouraged is an important practice that will strengthen you in the days to come.

Point to Ponder

God will keep the steadfast of mind in perfect peace; because he trusts in Him.[57]

Prayer for Power

Gracious God, help me to be alert and on guard as I journey. Strengthen me by the power of Your Spirit that I might encourage my brothers and sisters in Christ as we hold one another accountable in You. Blessed Lord, may we not isolate and forsake the assembling of ourselves together[58] but gather in the Spirit to the praise and glory of Your name, Amen.

Pursue your Purpose

As you remain alert in your purpose, the Holy Spirit will guide you to the encouragement of your family in Christ. Meditate on Hebrews 10:19–25

THE END TIMES

And he said with a loud voice, "Fear God, and give Him glory,
because the hour of His judgment has come; worship Him who
made the heaven and the earth and sea and springs of waters."
REVELATION 14:7

Every day of our lives is dedicated to fearing God and giving Him glory. As Christians, we fear God in the sense of reverence and veneration. As the hour of His judgment arrives, scripture gives us the sense that there will be terror, reverence, and veneration. Is your relationship with God one of terror, reverence, or both?

I remember the first time in my Christian walk when I felt the sense that God was angry with me. It was startling and unnerving. I was afraid. I cried as I felt a sense of what I termed "God's heartbrokenness" overtake me. I knew that this all-powerful God did not have to tolerate my foolishness. Then I felt His love enfold me and I knew everything would be alright.

God is the "same yesterday, today, and forever."[59] From "Let there be" to eternity, God will never change.

Point to Ponder

"God knows the way that you take; when He has tried you, you will come out as gold."[60]

Prayer for Power

Awesome God, maker of heaven and earth, I give you all praise, honor, and glory! My heart does safely trust in You. I yearn to know You more. Help me grow in my relationship with You, to not be terrified by Your greatness but to love Your appearing. In Jesus' name, Amen.

Pursue your Purpose

Have there been times in your journey when you have sensed the "heartbrokenness of God?" Been afraid of God? How have you reconciled these feelings with the lover of your soul? Meditate in 2 Timothy 4.

I WISH YOU COULD SEE
WHAT I SEE

I wish you could see what I see.
Fearfully and wonderfully made in the image of God;
More than a conqueror speaking truth to dried bones
watching them come alive.

I wish you could see what I see.
Destined and determined to be conformed
to the image of Me.
Walking in liberty, glowing with sanctity,
secure in My majesty

I wish you could see what I see.
Pure without wrinkle or spot,
showing the world what you've got
teaching them that they could have it too
if they seek the TRUTH

But, you don't see what I see.
Because if you did you would live free
delivered from the bondage of me, myself and I.
Fear tying your wings so you can't fly

Tying your wings so you can't fly,

tying your wings so you can't fly,
don't you wonder why you can't fly?
The devil is a liar.

Fear of seeing what I see
has disabled your wings.
Letting the enemy control you
with his puppet strings.
If you would only see what I see.

— LeSette M. Wright ©2001

Do you see yourself as God sees you? If not, it's time to start! God fashioned you in His image and likeness. He breathed the breath of life into you. You are beloved of the Most High God. When we look into the mirror of God's word, we should be encouraged and empowered by God's love for us! Fear has tied your wings for too long. It's time to fly! With God, all things are truly possible.[61] You will never be perfect in the frailty of your humanity but you are perfect in Him. Stay on the journey. When you fall, get up.[62] Press forward. God's will for you is good, perfect and acceptable. Embrace it.

Point to Ponder

When gazing into the mirror of God's word, the reflection of His love is brilliant!

Prayer for Power

God of healing and strength, You who have opened the eyes of the blind and caused the lame to walk. Open my eyes that I might see myself the way you see me. As I look into the mirror of Your word, may Your transforming truth meet my gaze and revolutionize my perspective. Thank you for revealing Your truth to me by the power of Your Spirit. In Jesus' name, Amen.

Pursue your Purpose

It's empowering to see yourself as God sees you. Spend time in the mirror. Meditate in Luke 10:17–24.

ARE YOU READY TO SOAR?

Have you ever been in a situation where you just felt stuck? No matter what you did you could not break free. There was something preventing you from moving forward. Preventing you from doing what you knew you needed to do.

Well, I hate to break it to you but that something preventing you from moving forward is you! Yes, you and your cesspool of excuses. Excuses stem from fear of doing what you know needs to be done. Fear of seeing you as God sees you. Fear limits your perspective to a box. If you look closely in this box you will find that it is filled with broken wings. Wings that you've allowed to be severed every time you permit fear to produce an excuse from your lips.

Now, I hear you thinking that some excuses are valid: I have kids to think about, a spouse, an elderly parent, student loans, a ton of debt. Or you may be saying, I don't have a college education, I don't know the first thing about starting a business, I'm too old, I have a family, I'm too young, I'm a Christian, I'm a housewife, I have a speech impediment, etc. Beloved, you must realize that as long as you have an excuse you will never reach your potential. As a matter of fact put down this book right now and get a piece of paper. Now write the following quote on the paper:

> *As long as a man has an excuse,*
> *he will never reach his potential.*
>
> — Lesette M. Wright

Now, put that piece of paper somewhere you will have to read it every day. On a mirror, the refrigerator, a door, your car dashboard, wherever. Remind yourself every day that there is no room for excuses in your life. The excuses must go. You must realize that there will always be reasons why you can't. Your challenge is to always find the reasons why you can.

You have heard the expression, "where there is a will there is a way." Well, I submit to you today, "where there is God's will the way is already made." Yes, God "knows the plans He has for us. Plans to prosper us and not harm us." Plans to give us hope and a future![63] You have allowed fear to tie your wings for too long. Aren't you ready to soar?

Somebody needs that book you have been wanting to write. Somebody needs that financial ministry you have been talking about starting. Somebody needs you to sing that song in your heart. Somebody needs you to share that testimony of how God blessed you. Somebody needs you to be their missionary to bring them the gospel. Somebody needs you to be a mentor in their lives. Yes, there is something in you that somebody needs. Release it and soar.

Point to Ponder

God has called you to soar "for such a time as this."[64]

Prayer for Power

Dear Lord, "they that wait upon You will renew their strength. They will mount up on wings like eagles. They will run and not be weary. They will walk and not faint."[65] May this character arise in me as I soar in my purpose. Forgive me for allowing fear to tie my wings. I now move forward in a renewed strength and clarity in You. In Jesus' name I pray, Amen.

Pursue your Purpose

Prayer, humility, a steadfast spirit, and Godly counsel are central in developing the skill to soar. Meditate in the book of Esther. What does her story teach you about soaring? Did Esther allow fear to tie her wings?

PART III

As You Learn His Ways,
Sing Your Song!

THE RAINBOW

Remember the story of Dorothy in the Wizard of Oz? As she sang *Somewhere Over the Rainbow,* Dorothy fantasized that somewhere over the rainbow was an abundant land; a land where dreams come true. When she found that land, she realized that what she needed in order to get home was with her all the time.

Well beloved, now is the time to wake up and realize that everything you need to get home has been deposited within you by Almighty God. He has called you to use it for such a time as this. The world needs you to wake up, to overcome fear, to attain the abundant life.

In Irish folklore, the leprechaun has a hidden pot of gold at the end of the rainbow. Perhaps, that pot of gold really is there; that pot of gold is the abundant life and God has it for each and every one of you.

Once you realize and take hold of your abundant life, share the rainbow with someone else. Through your testimony, through God's promises, and through this book, which is God's love letter to you! Be encouraged and enjoy the journey. There's a blessing in contrary winds.

The measuring rod of your abundant life is your obedience to God. If you have walked faithfully in Christ, you have walked in abundance. Success cannot be measured by material things and appreciation from man. God is the judge of your embracing the abundant life.

We began this journey together by crying out to God. As God answered us in each chapter we learned His ways and in experiencing His ways we can sing our song. "Sing a song of praise to the Lord, for He is your strength, your song and your salvation."[66] In Exodus 15, we partake in the songs of Moses and Miriam. We all have a song of praise, thanks, and adoration to our God. What is your song? I leave you with mine.

Point to Ponder

You will "sing out the honor of His name and make His praise glorious."[67]

Prayer for Power

Lord God Almighty, thank You for delivering me from a spirit of fear. You are an awesome God and worthy of all my praise. Help me to make Your praise glorious, to honor You in all that I am and all that I do. May Your rainbow remind me of the faithfulness of Your promise and surety of Your covenant with all those who love Your appearing. In Jesus' name, Amen.

Pursue your Purpose

Your pursuit of purpose is incomplete without praise.
Meditate in Psalm 66.

Thankful (Psalm 100)

Chorus:
How do I thank you for the love you've given me.
And how do I thank you for saving my life at Calvary.
Yes, how do I thank you for the love you've given me.
I just want to thank you.
I just have to thank you.
Oh Lord I give all praise to thee.

As I reflect on my life
There were many roads so dark and gray.
I was quick to take the broad path
That led to destruction and decay
But even in these times of trouble
When I lost my way
You were there to lead me out.
Even when my heart did doubt
Oh, Lord ,you never left me
Nor did you forsake me.
I'm so grateful to you my King.

Chorus

So many times I've asked myself
What manner of love is this?
For I know what I deserve
Yet you use me in spite of my mess.
And my heart cries Allelui.a

And my soul rejoices in thee.
Lord, I just want to thank you.
I die to self to serve you.
I'm so grateful to you my King.

Chorus

— Lesette M. Wright© 2001

Prayer

Dear God,

Your word says that You have come that I "might have life and have it more abundantly."[68] Thank You for the transformation that has occurred in my life over the last month. I stand firm in the truth that You have not given me a "spirit of fear but of power, love, and a sound mind."[69] I go forward in victory knowing that I am "more than a conquerer through Christ Jesus my Lord."[70] Gracious and loving Holy Spirit keep me on the path that brings glory to God. Help me with each passing moment to "press toward the mark of the high calling I have in Christ Jesus."[71] As I soar on eagles' wings, may I "dwell in the secret place of the most high God and abide under the shadow of the almighty."[72] Thank You that the best is yet to come! It is in Your name that I pray, Amen.

About the Author

Dr. LeSette M. Wright is a chaplain, mental health clinician, and professor with a commitment and passion for helping God's people live life more abundantly. With graduate degrees from Gordon-Conwell Theological Seminary, Temple University, and LaSalle University, Dr. Wright is the first Violence Prevention Minister for the American Baptist Churches of Massachusetts and the first African-American woman to be ordained to ministry from the historic Tremont Temple Baptist Church in Boston.

Dr. Wright is an internationally recognized speaker, trainer, and guest lecturer. Some of her topics include: Transformative Community Chaplaincy, Spiritual Formation and Discipleship, Fear Management/Resolution, Soul Care for Ministry Leaders, Anger Management/ Resolution, Self-care for Women, and Ministering God's Peace in the Upfront, In the Thick and Aftermath of Violence. Scheduling requests for Dr. Wright can be sent to: Lesette@seekthepeace.org or 609-277-3223.

Notes

1 2 Timothy 1:7 NKJV
2 John 10:10 KJV
3 Philippians 3:14 KJV
4 The origin of this acronym is unkown.
5 Jeremiah 29:11
6 Philippians 4:7
7 2 Timothy 1:7
8 Genesis 3:10 KJV
9 2 Corinthians 10:5 KJV
10 Philippians 4:13
11 Deuteronomy 31:6 KJV
12 John 3:16 KJV
13 Bold type added by author for emphasis.
14 Psalm 138:8 KJV
15 Colossians 3:2
16 Ephesians 2:10
17 Romans 12:2 KJV
18 Jeremiah 29:11
19 Romans 8:28
20 Author's paraphrase of Psalm 139:23–24
21 1 Peter 5:10
22 Romans 8:37
23 Joshua 1:5
24 1 Thessalonians 5:24
25 Deuteronomy 31:6
26 Acts 10:34
27 Romans 8:37
28 Joshua 1:9 NIV
29 Psalm 119:11
30 Joshua 1:8
31 1 Samuel 16:7

32 2 Corinthians 10:4
33 Ephesians 6:13–18
34 Ephesians 6:10–18
35 Proverbs 3:5–6
36 Acts 17:28
37 Proverbs 3:5–6
38 Ephesians 6:13
39 Philippians 4:13
40 Matthew 19:26
41 Matthew 7:13
42 Philippians 4:13
43 Psalm 103:10
44 Psalm 103:10–11
45 The author refers to a "stronghold of deservedness" as spiritual bondage that enslaves one to the idea that they must merit God's favor through personal works.
46 Psalm 90:12
47 John 14:6
48 John 8:36
49 Psalm 119:105
50 1 John 2:21
51 Matthew 25:21
52 Luke 1:38
53 Luke 21:26
54 Luke 21:28
55 1 Peter 4:18
56 Proverbs 11:14
57 Paraphrased from Isaiah 26:3
58 Hebrews 10:25
59 Hebrews 13:8
60 Job 23:10
61 Matthew 19:26
62 Proverbs 24:16
63 Jeremiah 29:11

64 Esther 4:14
65 Isaiah 40:31
66 Isaiah 12:2
67 Psalm 66:2
68 John 10:10
69 2 Timothy 1:7
70 Romans 8:37
71 Philippians 3:14
72 Psalm 91:1

Made in the USA
Columbia, SC
29 September 2018